MAKE YOUR OWN
BATH BOMBS

BY THE EDITORS OF KLUTZ

KLUTZ®

KLUTZ® creates activity books and other great stuff for kids ages 3 to 103. We began our corporate life in 1977 in a garage we shared with a Chevrolet Impala. Although we've outgrown that first office, Klutz galactic headquarters is still staffed entirely by real human beings. For those of you who collect mission statements, here's ours:

CREATE WONDERFUL THINGS · BE GOOD · HAVE FUN

WRITE US
We would love to hear your comments regarding this or any of our books.

KLUTZ®
568 Broadway, Suite 503
New York, NY 10012
thefolks@klutz.com

FSC™ MIX
Paper from responsible sources
FSC™ C113204
www.fsc.org

We make Klutz books using resources that have been approved by the Forest Stewardship Council™. This means the paper in this book comes exclusively from trees that have been grown and harvested responsibly.

Case marble texture and throughout © Berna Şafoğlu/Fotolia.

ISBN 978-1-338-15880-9
4 1 5 8 5 7 0 8

Baking soda made in the U.S.A. Fragrance and glass bottle manufactured in China. All other parts, Taiwan. Assembled in Taiwan. 85.

Ingredients/ Ingrédients
Baking Soda/ Bicarbonate de soude – Sodium Bicarbonate,
May Contain/ Peut Contenir (+/-): Red 7 (CI 15850), Yellow 5 (CI 19140), Blue 1 (CI 42090)

Citric Acid/ Acide citrique– Citric Acid

Fragrance/Huile aromatisée – Propanediol, Octadecanal, Linalool, Linalyl Acetate, Delta-decalactone, Ethyl Butyrate, Ethyl Propionate, Benzyl Alcohol

Glycerin/ Glycérine - Glycerin

Safety Information
Do not store bath bombs in air-tight containers.
Use only as directed; follow all directions in the book.
If swallowed, seek medical advice immediately. In case of contact with the eyes, rinse well with water.
Wash hands after making bath bombs. Discontinue use if irritation occurs.
If irritation persists, consult a physician.

Sécurité Renseignements
Ne pas ranger les bombes de bain effervescentes dans des contenants hermétiques.
Respecter les instructions d'emploi ; Suivre toutes les directives du livre.
Si des composants sont avalés, consulter immédiatement un médecin.
En cas de contact avec les yeux, bien rincer avec de l'eau.
Se laver les mains après avoir fabriqué des bombes de bain effervescentes.
Cesser d'utiliser ce produit en cas d'irritation cutanée. Consulter un médecin si l'irritation persiste.

Distributed in Australia by
Scholastic Australia Ltd
PO Box 579
Gosford, NSW
Australia 2250

Distributed in Canada by
Scholastic Canada Ltd
604 King Street West
Toronto, Ontario
Canada M5V 1E1

Distributed in Hong Kong by
Scholastic Hong Kong Ltd
Suites 2001-2, Top Glory Tower
262 Gloucester Road
Causeway Bay, Hong Kong

Visit this site to watch how we make our bath bombs!
klutz.com/bathbombsvideo

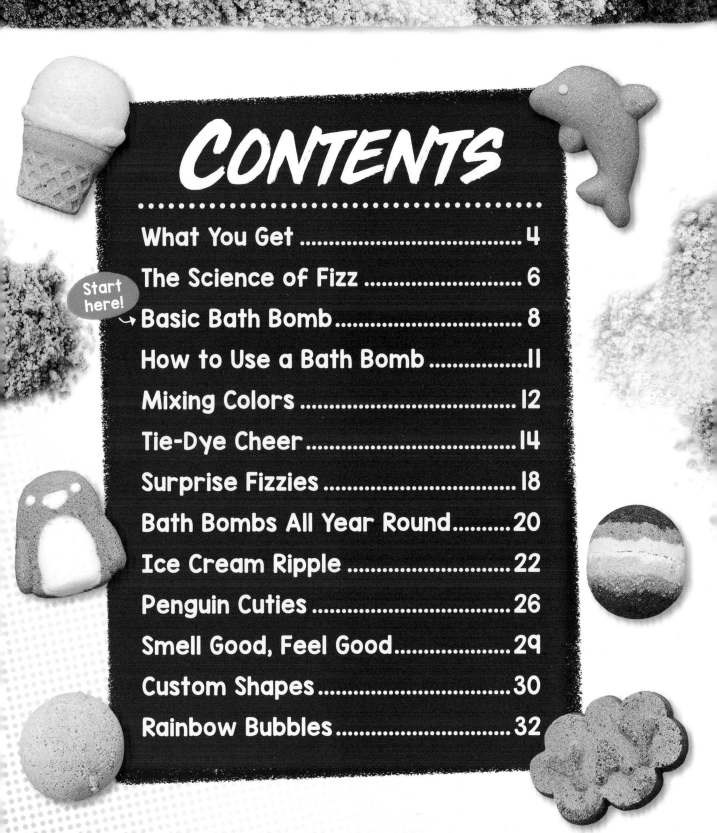

CONTENTS

Start here!

WHAT YOU GET

YELLOW
BAKING SODA

RED
BAKING SODA

BLUE
BAKING SODA

CITRIC ACID

5 MOLDS

STRAWBERRY KIWI SCENT

MAKE YOUR OWN Bath Bombs

GLYCERIN

MAKE YOUR OWN Bath Bombs STRAWBERRY-KIWI

GATHER UP THESE SUPPLIES, TOO!
- measuring spoons
- mixing bowl
- plastic fork or spoon
- access to a refrigerator
- baking soda from your kitchen
(ask a grown-up for help and wash tools after using)

WARNING!

Colored baking soda can stain hands and clothes. Wear your favorite crafting clothes that you are allowed to get messy. Wash your hands after you use the baking soda.

Cover your table with newspaper or a plastic tablecloth. Clean up any mess with a wet paper towel or cloth.

Bath bombs are NOT food! Don't leave these craft supplies where babies or pets might get into them. Always let your bath bombs dry someplace they won't get wet.

If you are sensitive to the ingredients in the strawberry kiwi scent, simply leave it out. You can replace it with another scented oil (page 29).

Citric acid can mess up your manicure. Wear gloves if you want to keep your nail polish looking fresh.

When you use a bath bomb (page 11) keep the bubbles away from your eyes.

the Science of Fizz

Fun Fact!
The bubbles in soda are also made from carbon dioxide.

Bath bombs create fizz thanks to a special chemical reaction. As long as they're dry, the baking soda (also known as sodium bicarbonate) and citric acid specks live peacefully side by side in the bath bomb.

When you add water, the water breaks up the molecules of the baking soda and citric acid. Along with breaking the molecules up, the water also allows new chemicals to form from these broken-up molecules. One of these new chemicals is carbon dioxide, which is a gas. We see this carbon dioxide as tiny bubbles on the surface of the water.

The baking soda and citric acid are the key ingredients in bath bombs. Always add twice as much baking soda as citric acid to get the most fizz. The fizz will help spread the relaxing fragrance and skin-softening glycerin throughout the bathwater. You'll see how quickly the fizz moves by how the water changes color. If you have different colors in your bath bomb, they will mix together in the water.

This book includes 36 tsp (177 mL) of baking soda. That's enough to make one of each project, plus some extras. These measurements are for baking soda only. You'll need citric acid and glycerin, too.

3 tsp (15 mL)

5½ tsp (27 mL)

4½ tsp (22 mL)

4½ tsp (22 mL)

14½ tsp (72 mL)

MIXING -YOUR- *INGREDIENTS*

When you measure ingredients, try to make sure that the powder is level. You can use a knife to scrape off any extra.

PRETTY GOOD.

PERFECT!

Store your bath bomb like it's a piece of soap. Don't leave it in the sun or on nice furniture. Do NOT store bath bombs in an air-tight container.

If it's rainy or humid where you live, dry the bath bomb in a refrigerator. Humidity can set off the fizzing reaction and result in lumpy bath bombs.

basic BATH BOMB

Start with this basic blue dolphin, and you'll be a master bath-bomb crafter in no time! It helps to read through all the steps first.

1 Pour the blue baking soda and the citric acid into a mixing bowl.

2 Mix them together until they are all blended.

The color of the mixture will change when you've mixed the glycerin all the way in. Notice that the dry powder is pale blue, but the combined mixture is bright blue.

3 Add a few drops of strawberry kiwi scent, if you want. Add the glycerin.

4 Mix and smush the mixture with both hands really, really well. You need to smush it for 2–5 minutes. Don't give up—you can do it!

Try clumping some of the mixture together in your hand when you think it's ready.

When the mixture holds together like this, then it's ready to be molded.

5 Scoop all the squishy sand into the mold, and press down firmly.

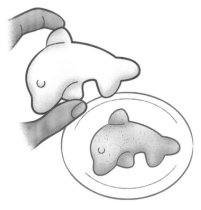

6 Let the bath bomb sit in the mold for **5 minutes.** Then gently turn the mold over onto a plate. Gently squeeze the sides of the mold to help it release. Or tap the back of the mold with a spoon or pen.

7 The bath bomb will fizz if you use it right away. But if you're giving it as a gift, let the bath bomb sit for **4 days** to fully dry.

TIP!
If it's rainy or humid, dry the bath bomb in a refrigerator. The fridge is a controlled, dry environment.

HOW TO USE A *BATH BOMB*

1 At bath time, fill up the tub with warm water. You can also use a jar with some water to test the reaction first.

2 Place your bath bomb in the water, and watch it fizz!

3 Step into the tub for a colorful soak. Don't splash the fizz on your face or eyes.

4 After you drain the water, clean up any color left in the tub.

MIXING COLORS

This book includes three colors of baking soda. You can make more colors with just red, yellow, and blue. We show you how to make 3 tsp (15 mL) of each color on these pages. The bath bomb you want to make might require more, so just measure out more until it matches the recipe.

RED
3 tsp (15 mL)
of red

YELLOW
3 tsp (15 mL)
of yellow

BLUE
3 tsp (15 mL)
of blue

PURPLE
1 tsp (5 mL) blue
+ 2 tsp (10 mL) red

ORANGE⤴
2 tsp (10 mL) yellow
+ 1 tsp (5 mL) red

GREEN⤴
2 tsp (10 mL) yellow
+ 1 tsp (5 mL) blue

BROWN⤴
1/2 tsp (2.5 mL) red + 1/2 tsp (2.5 mL) blue
+ 2 tsp (10 mL) yellow

Add white baking soda from your kitchen to make pastels.

PINK
$2\frac{1}{2}$ tsp (12.5 mL) white + $\frac{1}{2}$ tsp (2.5 mL) red

PEACH
$2\frac{1}{4}$ tsp (11.25 mL) white + $\frac{1}{4}$ tsp (1.25 mL) red + $\frac{1}{2}$ tsp (2.5 mL) yellow

BUTTERCUP
$2\frac{1}{2}$ tsp (12.5 mL) white + $\frac{1}{2}$ tsp (2.5 mL) yellow

MINT
$2\frac{1}{4}$ tsp (11.25 mL) white + $\frac{1}{4}$ tsp (1.25 mL) blue + $\frac{1}{2}$ tsp (2.5 mL) yellow

LIGHT BLUE
$2\frac{1}{2}$ tsp (12.5 mL) white + $\frac{1}{2}$ tsp (2.5 mL) blue

LAVENDER
2 tsp (10 mL) white + $\frac{1}{2}$ tsp (2.5 mL) red + $\frac{1}{2}$ tsp (2.5 mL) blue

TiE-DYE
Cheer

Make sure to mix the glycerin really, really well. The best way is to massage the mixture with your hands for 2-5 minutes until the powder turns bright and clumps together.

Any day of the week can feel like Fri-YAY when it ends with a nice soak in a groovy rainbow of colorful fizz. Oh, yeah!

What You'll Need

* YAY mold
* 2 tsp (10 mL) yellow baking soda
* 1 tsp (5 mL) blue baking soda
* 1½ tsp (7.5 mL) citric acid
* ¼ tsp (1.25 mL) glycerin (measure in drops, Step 4)
* Strawberry kiwi scent (optional)
* 2 separate mixing containers
* Plate

1 Add baking soda to each bowl.

Bowl #1 = 2 tsp of yellow

Bowl #2 = 1 tsp of blue

2 Add 1 tsp of citric acid to Bowl #1 (yellow) and ½ tsp to Bowl #2 (blue).

3 Mix the dry ingredients together.

TIP
If you want to make other colors, check out the ideas on page 12.

The color of the mixture will change when you've mixed the glycerin all the way in. Notice that the dry powder is pale but the combined mixture is bright.

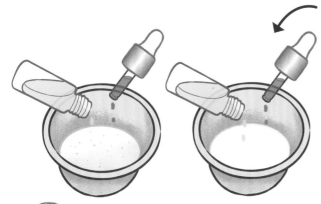

4 Add 12 drops of glycerin into the blue bowl. Add 20 drops of glycerin into the yellow. Add a drop of scent to each bowl.

5 Mix and smush the mixture with both hands really, really well. You need to smush it for 2–5 minutes. Don't give up—you can do it! Use the clump test on page 10 to check if your mixture is ready.

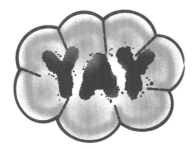

6 Sprinkle a bit of the blue to fill in the letters.

7 Randomly add all the remaining squishy sand to the mold, and press it all down.

SMELLY STUFF
Add two drops of scent to each bath bomb if you want enough scent to make 12 projects.

8 Let the mixture dry for **5 minutes,** then turn it over and unmold the bath bomb onto a plate. Squeeze the sides of the mold or tap the back with a pen, if you need to.

9 Set your plate somewhere it won't be disturbed for **4 days** to fully dry. Of course, you can pour it into your bath right away, and it will still fizz.

This project looks good as a solid color, too. Mix 3 tsp baking soda and $1\frac{1}{2}$ tsp citric acid, then add $\frac{1}{4}$ tsp of glycerin to make your mixture.

TIP
Dry the bath bomb in a refrigerator if the weather is humid or if it's rained recently.

Surprise fizzies

Hide a tiny toy inside a simple bath bomb to create a two-gifts-in-one bubbly ball of goodness.

You need to smush the mixture with both hands for 2-5 minutes. Use the clump test on page 10 to check if your mixture is ready.

Use the clump test on page 10 to check if your mixture is ready.

1 Mix the baking soda and citric acid. Add the glycerin and scent. Mix them until the pale powder turns into a bright colored mixture that clumps together.

2 Pack a little squishy sand in the bottom of one half of the mold.

3 Nestle a toy in the mold, and fill in the gaps with more mixture.

4 Pack the rest of the mixture into the other half of the mold and squeeze the two halves together.

5 After **5 minutes,** lift the top half of the mold off. Wait **4 days** to fully dry (in the fridge, if it's rainy or humid) before unmolding the other half.

*If you don't include a toy, add an extra 1 tsp baking soda, 1/2 tsp citric acid, and 4 drops of glycerin to fill up the mold.

BATH BOMBS
ALL YEAR ROUND

CANDY CORN

USE A PIECE OF PAPER
TO MAKE LAYERS [PAGE 24].

SNOWBALL

USE WHITE BAKING SODA AND
COSMETIC-GRADE GLITTER.

BE MINE

YOU CAN USE ANY FUN ICE CUBE
TRAY TO MAKE BATH BOMBS.
[ASK AN ADULT BEFORE YOU USE IT.]

BIRTHDAY SURPRISE

MIX A COUPLE OF DIFFERENT COLORS
TO MAKE A CONFETTI LOOK.

CHRISTMAS TREE

USE YOUR FAVORITE COOKIE CUTTER
(PAGE 31) TO MAKE A SEASONAL TREAT.

SPRING EGGS

MIX PASTEL COLORS (PAGE 13)
IN YOUR SPHERE MOLD.

Ice Cream RIPPLE

Sprinkles are safe to use in the bath, too! Put some in the mold before Step 1.

It's a single scoop cone that melts in the tub! Mix bright baking soda (pages 12-13) to create your favorite color.

1 Mix ½ tsp of red, 2 tsp of yellow, and ½ tsp of blue to make brown for the cone.

2 Add 1¾ tsp of citric acid and mix.

3 Add ¼ tsp of glycerin and a drop of scent.

Use the clump test on page 10 to check if your mixture is ready.

What You'll Need

* Ice cream mold
* 2 tsp (10 mL) yellow baking soda
* ½ tsp (2.5 mL) blue baking soda
* ½ tsp (2.5 mL) red baking soda
* 2½ tsp (12.5 mL) baking soda (for the scoop, your choice of color)
* 3¾ tsp (18.5 mL) citric acid
* ½ tsp (2.5 mL) glycerin
* Strawberry kiwi scent (optional)
* 2 mixing bowls
* Piece of paper
* Plate

The color of the mixture will change when you've mixed the glycerin all the way in. Notice that the dry powder is pale brown, but the combined mixture is dark brown.

4 Mix and smush the mixture with both hands really, really well. You need to smush it for 2–5 minutes. Don't give up—you can do it!

5 In a separate bowl, pour 2½ tsp of baking soda and 2 tsp citric acid, in your scoop color. Follow Steps 3–4 to make squishy sand.

6 Fold the paper and hold it in the mold to separate the scoop from the cone.

7 Add the brown squishy sand to the cone section of the mold. Add the other squishy sand to the scoop section of the mold.

TIP
If you're giving a bath bomb as a gift, wrap it loosely in tissue paper, and then in a gift box.

8 Remove the paper and gently press all the squishy sand down.

9 Wait **5 minutes** for the mixture to set. Then flip the mold over onto a plate. Gently squeeze the sides or tap the back with a spoon or pen.

10 Place the plate in a safe spot so the bath bomb can dry for **4 days.** You can use it a bit sooner if you handle it with care.

TIP
Dry the bath bomb in a refrigerator if the weather is humid or if it's rained recently.

Penguin CUTiES

This two-tone buddy is almost too adorable to use in a bath. Just remember that you can make this little birdie again and again.

1 Pour the white baking soda into a bowl.

2 Add 1 tsp (5 mL) of citric acid.

Use the clump test on page 10 to check if your mixture is ready. The mixture will also turn bright blue when it's ready.

3 Add 16 drops of glycerin and a drop of scent.

What You'll Need

....

* Penguin mold
* 1½ tsp (7.5 mL) white baking soda (from your kitchen)
* 3 tsp (15 mL) blue baking soda
* 3½ tsp (17 mL) citric acid
* ¼ tsp (1.25 mL) + 16 drops glycerin
* Strawberry kiwi scent (optional)
* Plate

4 Mix and smush the mixture with both hands really, really well. You need to smush it for 2–5 minutes. Don't give up—you can do it!

5 Press the white squishy sand into the belly of the penguin mold. Sprinkle some in the eye and beak details. Leave the white a little loose; don't pack it down too hard.

6 With the blue baking soda, 2½ tsp citric acid, and ¼ tsp glycerin, follow Steps 2–4 to make blue squishy sand.

7 Pour all the blue squishy sand into the penguin mold, and press it down with your fingers. Add leftover white squishy sand to the back if you like.

8 After **5 minutes,** turn the mold over to release the penguin onto a plate. If the white hasn't stuck to the blue, you can pack it back into the mold and release it again.

9 Let it dry for **4 days** to fully cure. If it's humid or rainy, pop the bath bomb into a refrigerator so it can dry in a controlled environment.

You can use vegetable oil instead of glycerin. Use a little more vegetable oil than glycerin—about 1 tsp of vegetable oil for every 3 tsp of baking soda.

We look awesome in different colors!

Smell Good, Feel Good

You can use essential oils (found in health-food stores) in place of the strawberry kiwi fragrance. Make sure that they are oils that are safe to use on skin. Different scents (and colors!) will affect your mood. Try using these oils if you're . . .

Feeling a bit blah?
VANILLA helps lift your mood. (Just like a vanilla-frosted cupcake!)

Preparing for a big game?
TANGERINE gives you energy and helps you concentrate.

Looking for sweet dreams?
LAVENDER helps make you sleepy and get a good night's rest.

Stressing out?
GREEN APPLE helps calm down any jitters. Smell ya later, stress!

Studying for a big test?
PEPPERMINT helps boost your brainpower!

CUSTOM SHAPES

I ♥ KLUTZ

Yep, you read that right. Raid the box of cookie cutters in your kitchen, and you can make any of the shapes into a bath bomb.

1 Set the cookie cutter on the paper plate.

Mix the glycerin into the powder with both hands for 2-5 minutes. Use the clump test on page 10 to check if your mixture is ready.

What You'll Need*

* **3 tsp (15 mL) baking soda** (your choice of color)
* **1½ tsp (7.5 mL) citric acid**
* **¼ tsp (1.25 mL) glycerin**
* **Strawberry kiwi scent (optional)**
* **Cookie cutter**
* **Plate**

*You may need more or less of these things if your cookie cutter is bigger or smaller than ours. We used a cookie cutter that was 2½ inches (6.5 cm) wide.

2 Mix the baking soda and citric acid. Add the glycerin and scent. Mix them until the pale powder turns into a bright colored mixture that clumps together.

3 Pack the squishy sand into the cookie cutter. Let it fully dry for about **4 days,** in the fridge if it's humid or rainy.

4 Gently press the bath bomb out of the cookie cutter.

Rainbow Bubbles

This poppin' project calls for a little extra patience. But hey, it's OK if your layers aren't perfectly even. Just enjoy the color party!

1 Pour 1½ tsp of red baking soda into a bowl.

What You'll Need

* Sphere mold (2 halves)
* 3 tsp (15 mL) red baking soda
* 7½ tsp (37.5 mL) blue baking soda
* 4 tsp (20 mL) yellow baking soda
* 6 tsp (30 mL) citric acid
* ⅔ tsp (3.5 mL) glycerin (measure in drops, Step 3)
* Strawberry kiwi scent (optional)

2 Add 1 tsp of citric acid to your bowl. Mix everything together.

Mix the glycerin into the powder with both hands for 2-5 minutes. Use the clump test on page 10 to check if your mixture is ready.

TIP
$3/_{11}$ tsp = ½ tsp + ¼ tsp

3 Add 16 drops of glycerin and a drop of scent into the bowl. Mix it in until you get squishy sand.

4 Pack all the red squishy sand into one half of the sphere mold.

5 Clean and dry your bowl and mixing tool before you move on to the next color. (This goes for every time you make a new color.)

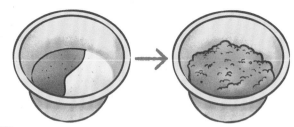

6 Pour ½ tsp of red and 1 tsp of yellow into a bowl and mix it to make orange. Follow Steps 2–3 to make squishy sand.

7 Pack all the orange squishy sand into the mold, adding it over the red layer.

8 Use 1½ tsp of yellow baking soda and follow Steps 2–3 to make yellow squishy sand. Pour all the yellow squishy sand over the orange layer, but don't press it down.

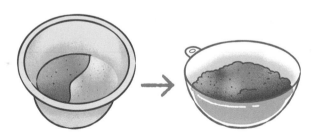

9 Mix 1 tsp of red and ½ tsp of blue baking soda in a clean and dry bowl. Follow Steps 2–3 to make purple squishy sand, and pack it all into the other half of the ball mold.

10 Use 1½ tsp of blue baking soda, and follow Steps 2–3 to make blue squishy sand. Pack it all on top of the purple layer in the mold.

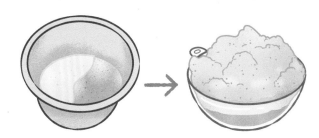

11 Mix 1 tsp of yellow and ½ tsp of blue. Follow Steps 2–3 to make green squishy sand. Pile all of it onto the blue layer, but don't pack it down.

12 Hold one half in each hand. Quickly bring them together so the green and the yellow layers smush together.

13 Carefully lift one half of the mold off. Let the bath bomb dry for about **4 days.** You can nestle it in a pile of confetti or an egg cup to keep it upright. If it's humid or rainy, dry it in a refrigerator.

TIP
If your bath bomb crumbles, that's OK! It will fizz like a regular bath bomb when you drop the pieces into water.

14 Once it's totally dry, gently remove the other half of the mold.

CREDITS

Editor: Caitlin Harpin

Designer: Kristin Carder

Technical Illustrator: Kat Uno

Buyer: Mimi Oey

Package Designer:
Owen Keating

Photographer:
Alexandra Grablewski

Stylist: Amanda Kingloff

Models: Jade C. and Logan S.

Fizzy Friends: F. S. Kim,
April Chorba, Armin Bautista,
Sam Walker, Emily Feliberty,
Kiffin Steurer, and Lizzy Doyle

The Bomb Dot Com:
Hannah Rogge and Netta Rabin

Bubbly Personality: Stacy Lellos

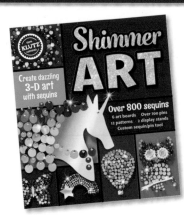
Visit this site to watch how we make our bath bombs!
klutz.com/bathbombsvideo